Learn**English**
WithAfrica

Learn English With Africa

B2 Short Stories in English

(Vol. 1)

Advanced Level

By
Thandi Ngwira Gatignol

CONTENTS

FOREWORD

This is a collection of eleven captivating short stories that are set in Africa and in the diaspora. The level is advanced in terms of vocabulary, grammar and the subjects that are dealt with.

In fact, this book features a wide range of thought-provoking themes that will broaden your mind and encourage you to read more books, not only about Africa, but about the world in general.

<u>Tips for getting the most out of a short story</u>
First, pay attention to the meaning of the story before focusing on vocabulary or grammatical structures.

Then, read the short story again and ask yourself the following questions: 1) What is the story about? 2) Who are the characters and what are their motivations? 3) What is the difference between the beginning of the short story and the end?

Lastly, write down interesting words, expressions or grammatical structures so that you can review them later. You will thus build your vocabulary and improve your English grammar in an active way.

I hope that this first collection of advanced short stories meets your expectations and fosters your own creativity.

Thandi Ngwira Gatignol, Founder and Author (Learn English With Africa)

The Language of the Heart
(with Vocabulary for Self-Talk)

My inner voice is my best friend and my worst enemy.

I mean, whoever lives inside my head has a hell of a time sending me contradictory messages. No wonder, nowadays I tend to disobey this voice more than I obey it, and it's perfectly all right with me. Hey voice, you have to know what you want! If you are behind the wheel, you have to give me clear instructions. Otherwise, I will just ignore you and do things my own way.

In fact, I've decided to ONLY listen to the voice that gives me good vibes. I tell you, this one is a gem. He or she, wait a minute, is this voice feminine or masculine? Well, I think it is a '*she*' since I am a young woman. So, coming back to our story, I must say that *she* creates such a lovely atmosphere inside my heart, or my mind, or both, and I have no trouble listening to her.

As a matter of fact, she is the one who tells me to wake up in the morning when the other one insists that I should stay in bed because it is warmer, isn't it?

"Wake up, dear." she says. "You'll be late for work. I know it's tough to leave your bed but if you wake up now, you won't be late and that's really good for your career." Whenever I hear this, I tend to wake up without any problems and I head straight to the bathroom.

Let me call this good voice of reason, Patience, because she is really patient with me.

The other side of my voice always has dark undertones even though she might be saying something apparently nice. "Stay in bed. Stay in bed. Who needs a promotion anyway? Just enjoy yourself."

She will say this over and over again until I give in. It's not even enjoyable when I stay in bed because I am overridden by guilt. I will call this version Sneaky because she always manages to sneak into the brighter crevices of my heart to turn off the lights so that I should lose my bearings.

Patience is kind; Sneaky is not unkind. I don't think Sneaky wants to hurt me, but her actions do hurt me so I think that I am better off without her.

The other day, I received a beautiful present from my co-workers. Patience was so happy for me. She kept telling me: "You deserve it Sarah. Enjoy this gift. You deserve it hundred percent."

My, my, my. You should have heard Sneaky's voice: "Sarah, ask yourself why these people are giving you presents. I don't want to disappoint you but I think it's because they want something from you. Or, it's their duty anyway to give you presents. Look, they give presents to everyone." Sneaky's nickname is '*Killjoy*', actually. She doesn't like to see me happy. This is why I absolutely want her out of my life.

The tricky thing is that Sneaky is so strong and over-powering and she tends to monopolise all conversations in my head. She loves monologues, as a matter of fact. You might say, why don't you tell her to shut up? Unfriend her like on Facebook or block her like on Twitter. She is useless anyway.

Well, I wish you were in my head and you would see what awful tantrums Sneaky throws when you don't acknowledge her existence. Telling her to shut up is the equivalent of snuffing life out of her. Telling her that she doesn't exist is like unlocking a bunch of snakes out of a thousand-year-old trunk. Gosh, she won't let me do that to her. Whatever the case, you wouldn't want to be in my head when hell breaks loose. Sneaky knows this so she keeps on sneaking up on me to disturb my peace.

Therefore, she becomes omnipresent after my futile efforts to quieten her a bit. She becomes more vocal to make up for lost time and I can't really do anything about it. Patience and I look just look at her and wait for her to calm down. Usually, I leave the scene. I walk away. I take a book or watch TV and dread the moment when I have to confront her again. Sneaky is sneaky and she never gives up. Even when I am watching TV, she tries to sneak into the story and I see her everywhere and I have to firmly tell her to leave me alone.

I know some people embrace the bottle so that they can drown Sneaky but my Sneaky is a good swimmer. I think she would swim across a brewery and emerge victorious anyway. I have found out that ignoring Sneaky is the best option. She gets really angry when I am not paying attention to her but afterwards she leaves me alone.

Anyway, I have better things to do than spending my life monitoring her and telling her what to do.

On the contrary, Patience always supports my decisions. She often tells me: "Don't worry, you are doing well. Don't give up, you'll make it. Wow, you look nice today, I like your outfit. Oh, my dear, you are feeling unwell, go to the doctor please before things get too bad. You are strong, you'll make it."

What does Sneaky say? She is like: "Oh, that mouth sore should be cancer. You're about to die. Oh, you look *sooooo* weak, stand up. You shouldn't look so weak. DON'T sleep! Keep working! You are the best. You can't **be** weak. Don't rest." Patience is unlike Sneaky. She quickly tells me to rest because it is important for the body to do so. "Be kind to yourself Sarah. You deserve to rest. You don't need to be the best. Go to bed and you will feel better in the morning."

Patience's tone is so soothing and nowadays I tend to follow Patience's instructions more than Sneaky's yelling. Before, I was scared of Sneaky and I would listen to her, ignoring the pain in my body in order to satisfy her every whim. Now, I listen to my body and I take care of it, whether Sneaky likes it or not.

The problem is that Sneaky makes a big deal out of everything. A small problem becomes a mountain for her and if I listened to her all the time, I tell you I would live in crisis mode all the time.

ME: Oh, I forgot to pay the bills, dear me.

Patience: You can pay the bills now; you still have some time. Just take out twenty minutes from your schedule and settle the bill.

Sneaky (First version): Pay the bill now! They are going to cut the electricity off! What are you doing? DO IT NOW.

Sneaky (Second version): Don't pay the bill now. You can wait a little bit. It's not like they are going to come and cut off the electricity. Some people can actually stay *FOR YEARS* without paying their bills and nothing happens to them."

And if something does happen to me when I have followed her bad advice, she is the first one to make me feel guilty: "Sarah, why on earth didn't you settle the bill when you still had time? You will always be a failure. Look at you, that's why you are always alone because people don't want to be with a person who is full of problems."

She can repeat this all day long and won't show any signs of stopping, even when I beg her to stop, even when she sees me crying, Sneaky won't relent. Gosh, I wonder why Sneaky even exists at all. All she does is criticise me day in, and day out, without bringing any positive aspect to my life. I really don't want to be in her vicinity anymore. Enough is enough.

This is why I have decided to empower **PATIENCE**. I give her more of my time and my attention. After all, *Sneaky* is just a voice, really. A voice! She doesn't even exist! I mean, she cannot come out of my body and physically harm me. I am the one who allows her to exist. Without my consent, she is absent. She, **really**, is absent. She is dead. Patience is present. Patience is the present. She is truly alive. I listen to her and follow her advice. I love her.

Whenever I catch a glimpse of *Sneaky* desperately trying to bring chaos to my heart, I look away and see

Patience's smile. She bolsters me; she's my pillar of strength. She soothes my heart with her empathetic vocabulary. Her grammar is simple and her punctuation clearly chartered. I can read her syntax and know exactly where I am. With Patience, I know I am in good hands.

A Blessing in Disguise
(with Synonyms and Antonyms)

The best creations are birthed through pain, Khama had gradually come to understand the nature of his journey as an artist.

It was a solitary trek with no immediate solace in sight but only the assurance that something good would always come out at the end of his quest.

There was nothing bad in trying, he knew. As long as he kept at his task, doing what he had to do no matter the hardship, always answering to the call of the universe, he would be all right.

Sometimes, he failed to comprehend the nature of the call. Why did he feel restless when he as much as deviated from his course for a single minute? For what reason did his heart beat so fast when he stopped believing in that calling?

Could he start to follow another path that would lead to another destination with different results? Was there something else he should do?

Deep down his heart, Khama knew that this walk would last him a lifetime. He had not chosen to take that walk. The walk had chosen him. Sometimes he wished he could shake off the burden and walk away. Yet, he knew that this was his calling. It entailed courage, boldness, perseverance and sacrifice for the common good.

He walked on, despite feeling the weight of the world bruising his shoulders. Often, he carried on, come rain or sunshine, despite the violent and silent opposition that aimed to crush his spirit so he could abandon his quest. Always, he braved the storms, wishing he couldn't, so he should experience peace at last and at least for a single second.

He thought about all the obstacles that had been and were still in his way. Some had been placed there voluntarily and these had tested his will the most. They continuously tried his patience and he had to muster up all the courage in the world in order to continue his journey. With time, he realised that these challenges were there for a reason.

As a matter of fact, each time he overcame an obstacle, he felt stronger and he could undertake his duties with resolute determination. His best work had come out of his worst moments and each difficult situation had always lead him to tremendous growth.

Yet, he did not want to experience mental and physical torture in order to grow and create. Why did it have to be so difficult? Why did it have to be so painful?

He dreaded those moments when he felt deafening earthly opposition in his midst. These were trying periods that repeatedly brought him to his knees. Often, he kept running unless he faltered. Others would sit down and accept defeat but he never did for he was sure that the worst would happen if he as much as stopped trying.

Each morning brought a new surprise, good or bad, and each evening birthed a novel idea, wonderful or awful. Yet, he always woke up with purpose because he had learnt that doing was demanding. You needed to be on your guard, right from the start, because you never knew what thorns lay in your path.

He spent many a sleepless night thinking about what would come next. Worrying was out of question though. Many a painful lesson had taught him that worries brought about misery. You needed to have a light, clean and an uncluttered spirit in order to carry out the job. You could not do what was right if your heart was heavy and laden with unproductive thoughts.

Whenever he felt a cloud of negativity hovering above his head, he summoned the winds of benevolence and blew that negativity away with a blast. Whenever he felt his legs weakening at the thought of yet another hard day, he recalled his past deeds and how they had been beneficial to others and to himself. Then, he became convinced that strength, and not weakness, was what needed to be infused into those legs so he could keep doing what was right.

His creations were meaningful and it was meaningless to stop creating, even when he did not reap immediate rewards. There is meaning in doing a job that we perceive to be rewardless yet it is rewarding in many other unseen ways.

Miraculously, he did not earn much money but he never went to bed hungry. No huge sums of money graced his bank account, yet he did not walk barefoot. He was fully clothed, nicely housed and managed to do his creations, even though his hands never received any wad of cash from anyone.

There was a satisfying mystery in knowing that he was being taken care of despite the lack of care and support that he perceived. Certainly, there was light in the darkness and power in being powerless.

Paradox was the nature of his job. He was doing something he chose to do every single day, yet he felt that he had not chosen to follow that path. Happiness lit his heart at each finished creation, forgetting the sadness that had led to its conception.

Pain jolted him into action, brought about the necessary urgency that pushed him to undertake what he would normally ignore in normal times. Pain forced him to stop and contemplate situations with a patient heart. Pain slowed him down and quickened his pace at the same time.

He had to accept the relentless pain so he could create outstanding beauty. Perfection was always carved out of a broken heart and the remedy to a sore spirit is to feed it with unspeakable beauty. Beauty heals the soul.

Magnificence is the medicine that cures a maimed mind and memory. Once the soul is healed, we can feel indescribable joy.

Mangoes for Lydia
(with the Simple Past Tense)

Lydia knew we were going to the lake for our Christmas holidays. Lydia didn't know we were going there *without* her. No one knew how to tell her to stop packing her bags; she wasn't coming with *us* after all. No one had the courage to break the news to this excited girl who had never set her foot on a beach before. It would be her first time, she shouted, and she was planning to enjoy herself to the fullest!

We didn't let her excitement dampen our spirits. We tried our best to share her joy even though we knew sorrow would replace it in the end. We talked about our future trip as if she were fully part of it. We talked about what we would do in Mangochi. We spent hours planning our meals. We salivated at the thought of eating fresh fish every day. We saw ourselves dripping with cool water as we emerged from the delicious expanses of the lake. We felt cold Fantas running down our throats as we waited for our dinner which would be brought to us by a real cook.

Lydia marvelled at our stories. Could we really drink as much Coke as we wanted? Would we bring full bags of baobab fruit back home? Could we share the bounty with our friends as we boasted about our real and imaginary adventures? Would we really sleep in a 'cottage', on clean white bedsheets and clean white pillows? Was it true that we could wake up whenever we wanted? Did we just say that there wouldn't be any housework for her? No housework?

Her questions never stopped and we answered them without restraint. We gave her comprehensive accounts of the houses we usually slept in. We described the contents of the fridges and our plates. We told her she could have anything she wanted once we arrived there. We gave her tiny details of unimaginable things and Lydia believed us without any hint of doubt. Our hearts were momentarily soothed. Each generous description chipped away at our guilt. We wanted to tell her the truth but the lies kept coming in and we couldn't stop them, *wouldn't* stop them.

Lydia's happiness grew as we neared our date of departure. We watched her pack and unpack her travelling bag, taking out sundry items and replacing them with new ones: a second-hand swimming costume, a notebook full of newspaper clippings of the lake, a second-hand bowler hat that she had bought from a street vendor in Limbe, *pata-patas* or plastic flip flops and two empty plastic bags in which she would put all her souvenirs. My sister and I looked away when she put her brown tattered bathing towel on top of her meagre belongings. We wondered how she would have been able to take that *out* in public, if she was coming with us.

'Why aren't you excited like me?' she asked us, puzzled that we didn't show off our enthusiasm. Really, who wouldn't be happy at the prospect of spending one's holidays on the lakeshore? We did not provide any explanations so she attributed our sighs to boredom and fatigue.

The night before we left, our mother came into our bedroom. Warmth filled my body at the thought of freeing myself from that heavy burden that had been encumbering me for days.

"Don't forget your swimsuits," my mother said.

"We won't Auntie," Lydia replied, her face beaming. "Look Auntie, my bag is already packed. I hope I haven't forgotten anything." She then stood up and embraced my mother, hugging her so tight and not letting her go for what seemed to us like ages. "Thank you Auntie, no one else would have done that for me. You are an angel."

I saw my mother squirm and fight to free herself from the uncomfortable position she had been locked into. When she finally stepped away, I found my sister staring at me and our eyes locked for a few seconds. I wrenched mine away from hers when I could no longer handle her pain. My mother left the room, reminding us once again to take everything we needed for our big trip.

At breakfast, my father chose to drink his tea in his bedroom. He hadn't slept well, he said. He needed to recover because he would be the one driving, wasn't it true? The soft cushy chairs of our dining room felt like they had been filled with prickly thorns overnight. We writhed and twisted and we hurried through our rituals in deafening silence. I spilled milk on my mother's favourite tablecloth and she said nothing. My sister drank her coffee with her eyes buried into a magazine. Even Lydia's usual chatter had disappeared, making room for this agonising silence that seeped into the food we ate and left deposits of shame in us. We felt the silence coursing through our entire bodies, gripping us in its jaws, tearing us apart and we looked at each other, helpless to stop it from breaking our family apart. We let cowardice over-whelm us, and rule us, and dictate what we had to do and *not* do to each other and to *ourselves.*

We let cowardice become us.

We let cowardice follow us to the car with Lydia trailing behind us with her fully packed travelling bag. We let circumstances decide our cousin's fate when 'there wasn't enough room' for her belongings. We let Lydia linger outside the door as she waited for us to make more room for her, she was finally coming with us to the lake, wasn't she? After long interminable minutes, we let Lydia understand and *decide* for *herself* that she wasn't coming with us after all, 'there wasn't enough room in the car for everyone.'

We felt relief, and unrestrained joy, when she finally uttered the words we all wanted to hear: "I will come with you next time, it doesn't matter."

"Really?" My father almost jumped out of his seat.

My mother went out of the car and engulfed Lydia with a huge hug. We saw Lydia's limp limbs as she failed to return the embrace. My mother's huge frame clasped her still. We looked away when we saw tears running down Lydia's cheeks. We looked away when my mother did not wipe those tears away.

"Wait a minute Lydia. You are a brave girl," our mother finally said.

We let our eyes follow my mother's figure as it went behind the car and opened the boot, taking out a big bag of ripe mangoes.

"Here, take all this. This is all yours."

We hoped that Lydia would jump with delight, mangoes were *her* favourite fruit after all. We instead saw Lydia's lifeless hands receiving the bag. We later learnt that she had given all its contents to our neighbour's children. Lydia.

We saw her standing slightly crouched as our car pulled away. Her eyes seemed to look beyond us. My father turned on the radio and we never talked about Lydia during the whole trip to the lake.

When we came back, we hoped that Lydia would be angry with us so we could eliminate our guilt in peace. Lydia welcomed us and did everything she could do to make ourselves feel comfortable. She was younger than us but she continued to wash our clothes, cook for us and wash dishes for us. We continued to tell her our stories and she listened, giving a piece of advice here and there, laughing when she had to and getting offended when required. We continued to behave as if nothing had happened.

Nonetheless, Lydia had changed. Her face was covered with a tiny rash that refused to go away despite the myriad of lotions and medication that we smeared on her face every day. Lydia became less talkative too, preferring to spend more and more time on her own. She also sang quite a lot and we told her to stop doing that because we were annoyed by the noise she made.

One day, we found her gone. She had taken all the things she had brought from the village, leaving behind everything she had acquired during her stay with us in Blantyre. She had not left any explanatory note. My father did not report her disappearance to the police, these things happened all the time, didn't they?

A letter arrived from Lydia's mother after six months. She was apologising for her daughter's lack of gratitude. How could she run away, really, after all we had done for her? She reassured my father that Lydia had been well taken care of for her rudeness, she was sure not to repeat such despicable mischief again. Finally, as usual, she also asked for money from us which my father readily sent. The cleansing had been done. The future was up for grabs, but strangely enough it didn't look promising.

I am telling you all this because we just buried Lydia a few days ago after a long illness. Her two sons chose to remain in the village: their mother had left them a house and enough money to pay for their secondary school fees. Lydia didn't want to leave them in a state of dependence, of utter helplessness. I insisted that her two sons come with me. I live in a huge house and I can send them to private schools. They refused my generous offer. They prefer to stay in the village. This is where they were born and who said the village was a bad place?

My sister and I cried so much at Lydia's funeral and her sons had to prop us up. Mourners forgot who were the real bereaved family, I am ashamed we made such a ruckus and a fool of ourselves. We were surprised by Lydia's sons' strength and poise; we were surprised by their wise nature despite their loss. They looked so comfortable in their skin, any one could tell they didn't need *anyone*, they didn't need *us*, they didn't need *me*.

I would have liked to tell you that Lydia had triumphed over us in many ways. I would have liked to tell you a different story of how Lydia became a doctor or a lawyer, beating all odds after she had left our family. None of that happened. Stories like that are mostly found in books. We are talking about real life here; we are talking about real lives.

I wished I had gone to see her when she was ill. I wish we had talked about what happened during those Christmas holidays when everything changed, yes, even in our own family. I will spare you the details.

I wish I had gone back to the village and taken Lydia with her family to the lake. I imagine her stepping into the cool water, walking farther and farther, taming the waves and finally steeping her full body into such magnificence, splashing and squealing with childish delight, letting the deep blue waters of Lake Malawi envelop her into their warm and nurturing embrace.

Outbound

(with Interrogative Pronouns)

He left yesterday. There were no goodbyes. What for? Why should you say goodbye to someone who is never coming back? That's what my mother said. Let him go. Let him fend for himself. Let him go. Let him go. Let him go. Full stop.

My mother did not cry when he left. What for? She said. How can I shed any tears when there are none left? It is anger I feel, she repeated. I have cried enough tears to fill a hundred wells. There is nothing else I can do. My son is gone and I cannot do anything about it. I cannot do anything about it. I cannot do anything about it.

He took a small bag and filled it with what he could salvage from his bedroom: a few clothes, a pair of shoes and some books. Our neighbour gave him roasted maize and groundnuts for the trip. He wasn't taking much on purpose. There was a lot more waiting for him at his final destination. Why fill his bag with rubbish when there were better things for him abroad?

Where was he going? He didn't know. What was he going to do there? He didn't know. Why was he leaving us? He knew. This was the only thing he was sure about. He did not tell us why.

My father saw him leave. He didn't talk to him. Why would he? He asked. There was nothing to tell a stubborn will. There is nothing to tell a goat that has decided to rush to its own destruction. There is nothing to tell such a will.

He was smiling when he left-yes, he was. The people who were there told me. He wasn't afraid, no, he wasn't. They said his face shone bright as his future. They could already picture him coming back with a Mercedes-Benz and 10 smart phones for each of his fingers.

My brother is a dreamer. He likes building mansions in his head.

I didn't see him leaving. I didn't want to. Why? What's the use of holding onto thin air?

Perhaps I didn't want to see the look of hurt on my father's face. Perhaps I didn't want to see my brother's smug expression as he left for the unknown. Perhaps I didn't want to envy him. The fact was he was chasing his dreams. Was I courageous as he was? Maybe it wasn't all about courage? Maybe it was just pure recklessness. How would I ever know?

He swaggered to the bus stop, my brother. He didn't know where he was going, silly him. He didn't know what he was leaving behind, what a pity!

My mother spent the whole day between the borehole and our house. We now have plenty of water in the drum.

She said she wasn't going to let her anger consume her. She said she didn't have time that. He has chosen to go, hasn't he? Let him go. Let me go. Let him go. My life will continue. Full stop.

My father is at the bottle store since my brother left, yes he is. My mother said let him stay there. Let him drink. Let him drink. Let him drink. He will come back when the bottle has become his enemy. As for now, they can still be friends. As for now.

I slept at my friend's house, I did. I needed some peace. Who wants to stay in a sinking ship? No one.

The fields are waiting for us. They can wait. They can wait. They can wait. What with one less mouth to feed-it doesn't matter anymore. It doesn't matter. It doesn't matter. It doesn't matter-matter.

My mother wants to hear none of our nonsense. Our life should never stop. People choose to do what they want to do. Full stop.

She knows whom she can point her finger at. The useless bananas, she calls them. Useless bananas who have stolen hope from her son.

We are going to spend the next years waiting. We will strain our eyes to capture the fleeting image of our brother. We will open our ears wide to capture any news about the almost forgotten brother, the almost forgotten son. Maybe one day we will stop waiting. Maybe one day he will come back. Maybe one day we will forget that this ever happened. Is this wishful thinking? I hope not. They never come back, do they? They get lost and no one ever hears about them. They are gone, gone forever. Forever, they are gone.

He promised us wealth. He promised us a better life. He said we would no longer suffer. Pain will just be a memory, he said. A distant memory.

He doesn't know, my mother said. He just doesn't. How can he know the pain of a mother? He will never know. He will never, ever know. HER son will never know.

Our country is beautiful. Look at our lush vegetation. Look at our fertile lands. Look at our gushing rivers. What a blessing!

My mother sighs.

Look at me. I am still alive. I am a healthy and loving mother.

Look at his father. He is still alive. Has he ever failed to guide our son through life?

Look at you. You are his sister. You are still alive. Will your brother ever attend your wedding? Will he ever, ever see your first born son?

Why would anyone leave a place where he knows everybody to go to a place where he knows nobody? Why would he?

My mother cannot understand.

Neither can I.

But to each his own.

My mother did everything she could to keep him. He shut his ears to my mother's pleas. He shut his eyes to my mother's weight loss. He shut his heart to my mother's distress.

She fasted. She entreated him. She fed him like a king. She threatened him. She said nothing.

Her fasting could not change his mind. Her shaved head could not change his mind. My brother's mind was made up. He wanted to go. No one or nothing could make him change his mind. HE had decided to go.

My Daughter from France
(with Adjectives for Describing Feelings)

My daughter came back a few weeks ago speaking another language. Not Chichewa, not Chiyao, not English, as you would probably imagine since she went to France. *Bonjour Papa*, were the first words she said when she saw me after five whole years. She did not kneel down as it is our custom. She did not drop her eyes onto the floor, averting her gaze, as our ancestors would require. No, she looked straight at me with her charcoaled eyes, painted lips and sleek hair, a bright red handbag dangling from her bare arms, her feet squeezed into pointed steel shoes. I could almost hear NyaChirwa's strangled groan from her grave.

"*Bonjour Papa*," she repeated when she saw my narrowing eyes. "Aren't you happy to see me?"

You see, my daughter left us during the year of the drought. I think you all remember that time when the maize refused to grow and our thin cattle refused to live, falling one by one like Vimbuza dancers. You know the year when the river dried and we could see its bare intestines. It was the year when NyaChirwa and many others left this world, the year when we had to find another graveyard to welcome all those departed, wrenched from our hands by the fatal alliance between hunger and Aids. This was also the year Tamara decided to leave us, only to return as this cheap, diluted version of herself, a stranger in her own land, a stranger to her own ways. For all I know, the Tamara I knew left with that senseless drought that robbed us of all we ever had.

The Tamara I knew will never come back. The Tamara I knew is gone forever. The Tamara I know now goes into people's homes and lectures them on how they should live, how they should dress, how they should eat, how they should treat each other. She says that it is not normal to see children running around in bare feet. She says it is inhuman to let them walk in torn clothes and wallow in dirt. She even says that men should help their wives everywhere, even in the kitchen. She has seen it done in Europe, why not here?

"Those old days are gone *Papa. On doit s'adapter au monde moderne.* We have to adapt ourselves to the modern world." This is why her respect has become conditional: those who produce deserve her attention, those who don't, even if they can't, are given her utmost contempt. Why? When she left five years ago, she never did such things, never asked such questions, never back-talked to me or shouted nonsense at elderly people for that matter. What has happened?

Perhaps it is because of her man-friend who calls her every day on her cellular phone as if she was the most important thing in the world. Every day, without fail. I can tell that she has fallen stupidly in love with this man, from the way she stops doing whatever she was doing in order to take his call. They speak in that foreign language for ages and I cannot even understand a single word.

My daughter has really changed. She has got odd habits that make people laugh and shake their heads but I cannot help feeling sad for her. Can you imagine that she refuses to eat *sima* in the afternoon because she says she is on diet? Ha! Has she forgotten how we almost died for lack of food during that fateful year? And now she says that she wants to have a flat stomach. There are too many carbohydrates in *sima*, it's bad for the tummy. NyaChirwa *mama we*, listen to your daughter talking. Shut her mouth with your sharp talk that I remember too well. Scream from that clay hole and let your extinguished voice bring common sense to your daughter. Let that dry earth wring out its disapproval.

My daughter from France just drinks bottled water, like the type we sell to tourists, I am telling you the truth. She thinks that our borehole water is contaminated. I would have said that this was the work of witches if she had been in this country. But it is common fact that those people do not practise common sorcery. What can you make out of those aeroplanes, cellular phones, cars and all their inventions?

Instead of spending her time going to fetch water, she says that she is on holiday. She says that the men of the village should have invented a device that would free their wives from such a gruelling chore. She says that the women deserve to rest. "They are also human beings *Papa*. They also deserve to sit and rest on the verandah like you do in the afternoons. They are not machines or beasts of the field *Papa. La vie est trop courte Papa.* Life is too short. One day those women will wake up and ask themselves where their life has gone."

She thus takes her camera and goes around in the village, taking pictures of people, telling them to stand this way and smile that way. She even photographed NyaKumwenda's skinny dog. Why would she do that? I thought cameras were meant to capture beauty. We put on our best clothes for the photographer. Why would she want to immortalise indignity? She says that these are the photos her friends back in France want to see. "Eyes are happy when they see something new *Papa.* Variety is the spice of the world."

Sometimes she talks to plants, whispering, and even stroking the leaves, as if they were human beings. "We have to be gentle with nature." This is why she glares at me when I bring back stacks of wood from the hills for our cooking. "What father's doing is really wrong. He just takes without giving back." I do not know if this was deliberately said in a loud voice so that I could get the message. This is not right. What should I do? What can I do? She eats raw food instead, insisting that it is good for her health. She ignores the symptoms of her recklessness. "It's normal *Papa.* It's just a matter of time. My bowels will get used to this."

Ha! NyaChirwa, I can now see how strong and resilient you were. You braved it all in that smoky, tiny kitchen that collapsed barely a month after your burial. *Chiuta mwe,* what a stiff punishment you dished out to me when you took my wife away. NyaChirwa! You were my pillar, my strength, my angel on earth. What a cruel lesson you taught me NyaChirwa with your untimely departure.

I have learnt, NyaChirwa, the hard way, but I have learnt what it feels like to be a village woman. I have tried to carry metal pails full of water on my head. I have tried to cook in the dark. I have pounded bags of maize in the mortar, looked after Mwiza day and night, swept, mended and traded. It is difficult NyaChirwa, it really is. I don't know how you managed it all. I have cried. I have cried from sorrow and I have cried from rage. I have also cried from utter hopelessness.

I will carry on though, NyaChirwa, I will, with dignity and pride. I still honour your memory NyaChirwa, I still do. It grieves me to see how my daughter is no longer the Tamara I knew. She has not become a bad person. No. She brought us a lot of medicine, bandages and food. I could open a small shop with all that she gave us. She sends me money though Western Union even though she lives so far away. She has not forgotten us. No. She still remembers our poverty. It would have been perfect if she had kept her original behaviour while doing all these good acts. At least, I would not feel as if the heavens had fallen on my head.

I tried to talk to her to understand why she has become another person, but she did not give me a satisfactory answer. The family that took her away from us, turning her into a five-star maid, is not to blame either. At first I did not understand why they never called us, why they never wrote to us, why they never bothered to know Tamara's family, Tamara's customs. With time,

I understood. Why would they? We are too different. Why would they want to talk to a useless old man like me? What do I have to offer them? What do we have to offer them? Our broken pots? Our empty stomachs? Our cracked limbs? Our sorrow-laden smiles? Tamara was enough to serve them, they didn't want any further burdens.

She now thinks that their lifestyle is better than ours so she copies everything that she sees. "Imagine *Papa*, electricity is all over the place, even in remote villages where my boss's parents live", she boasts. "We have machines that wash and dry clothes; big toys that clean the house; magic doors that spread wide open without anyone touching them." She goes on and on about this land that she calls Eden on earth. She can live on honey or milk, if she wanted. There are shops that are as wide as a mini-football ground. "You can have anything you want there. Anything *Papa*."

What about the people? Were they kind to her? "It's different there. Everyone minds their own business. In health or in sickness, the motto is fend for yourself. I really like that *Papa*." Poor Tamara. She does not know yet. You can get on by yourself with Malaria. When those pitiless afflictions such as Aids strike you, the warmth of another human being is more than welcome. When old age knocks at your door, robbing you of your strength, another man's words are not wasted. She does not know that yet so she can brag about a gossip-less free life where she can fulfill her dreams.

What about the people who were sent back home unceremoniously? Mr Nyirongo's son was now locked up in a tiny mud hut, afraid to show himself to the world in his cloak of tattered dreams. Wasn't she afraid that the same thing would happen to her? No, my daughter from France says she felt safe. Of course, some people were not so kind to her, in supermarkets for example. She always managed to find an escort in the name of a uniformed guard, who accompanied her through the aisles, checking if she was not slipping a deodorant into her handbag. On buses or in queues, people inched away from her automatically, even when she was well dressed and smelled nice. She was enraged by such cheap suspicion but that was all right *of course.* The constant humiliation was a small price to pay.

It was that or Aids, or hunger, or poverty, or the insecurity at home. She was ready to brave the permanent feeling of being an intruder, of being unwanted, of being expected to play cheaper and lesser roles even though she knew that she could do much better. When she put herself into her hosts' shoes, her predicament became a lighter burden to carry. What dignified person leaves her burning house without repairing it and seeks permanent shelter in her neighbour's home?

Oh, Tamara, my daughter from France. I don't know if I could live such a life. Are material things enough to mend a broken heart? Are material things enough to patch broken relationships? Are material things enough to bandage the wounds of a maimed country? I do not have the answers.

The day when my daughter lives for France is slowly approaching like judgment day. I feel the weight of her departure on my heart. I know that this could be the last time I might see her. My brother suggested that I should keep her passport so that she never goes back. I am still weighing this option. This would be the easiest solution. Or I could have some rich person marry her. But where will I find him? What will I do with her? What will I give her?

Force will be the only way to obtain what I want. If she remains home, then gradually like the change of seasons, that powerful influence will disappear. She will come back to us. She will be just like us. But I just cannot decide to do such an extreme act. I am afraid she will never be able to forgive me. I cannot live with her wrath over my head. I wish I had straight answers but I do not. I know NyaChirwa would have been able to help me. I talk to her, more than often, and people think I am losing my mind. Am I?

I cannot bring myself to go to her bedroom, search among her expensive belongings until I find what I am looking for. And I just realised that if I keep her with me, where is the money going to come from? I have to choose between bread and my daughter, between her presence and her presents, between respectability and love. It is such a difficult choice to make. Help me NyaChirwa.

Unconditional Love

(with Conditionals)

Her first son left while she was asleep. He didn't want to see his mother when he stole out of the village, penniless but filled with hope. When she woke up, he was gone. "If only I hadn't slept," she admonished herself bitterly, I would have said goodbye to my son. Now, he is gone and I will never see him again."

Her second son left while she was at the market. She had gone there to buy food for the whole family, including him. "If I leave now," he told himself, "she will not see me leaving and she won't be heartbroken." He snuck past the stalls of busy women and waved them goodbye. He never caught sight of his mother and she never caught a glimpse of her son. "If I had stayed a little bit longer at home, I would have hugged him for the last time. Now he is gone and I will never see him again."

Hence, she swore that she would keep her last son. She would guard him jealously and he would not even think of stepping out of the compound. She warned him of all the dangers he could encounter on his way to nowhere. He listened and nodded and swore in return that he would always remain in the village. The official mother of three smiled and lowered her defences. If only she could read people's minds! Once her grip was loosened, there was no way she would continue to detain him.

Empty promises! Empty promises from a son! If somebody decides to do something, they do it. You can never stop anyone from doing what they are dying to do. That's the nature of life and there is nothing she could do about it. The slap came sooner than she'd expected —unconditional love!

Her third son left while she was in the kitchen. She was preparing his favourite food: chicken with rice. "If I go now, the food will comfort her. I need to leave now, just like my brothers did. There is no future in this country, my mother will understand. She has unconditional love for me. If I were rich, I would stay here. I would build her a beautiful house and buy her stunning clothes that she truly deserves. I have nothing to give her. If I have nothing to show for my love as her one and only son, I cannot bear to see her suffer."

She saw him leave. His walk was different. It was as if he was running away from something, from someone. Instinctively, she knew. She knew deep down her heart that that he would not be coming back. "What wrong have I done?" she asked herself, holding her womb and feeling its empty promises lashing at her. "What wrong have I done? Was there anything I could have done to keep him? Didn't I give him unconditional love?"

"You did," her husband told her. "Look at all the hours you spent taking care of them. Wasn't that unconditional love?"

"It was my duty as a mother. I had to take care of my children and ensure that they were safe and healthy. I loved them."

"You showered them with love and never asked for anything in return," her own mother told her. "Isn't that unconditional love?"

"I don't know. I wanted them to stay. I didn't want them to go away. Look, I am now lonely. If I had money, I would travel around the world to see where they are. I would give everything that I had in order to see them again. I want to see my children again." She gripped her womb and tore at it carelessly. "It is as if this…this thing… never carried anyone. If I could see one of my sons again in my lifetime, I would be the happiest woman on earth."

Her last son came back while she was asleep. It was in the middle of the night. He stole past her bedroom and went to sleep in his former bed. She woke up and found the yard entirely swept. There was tea and bread with butter on the reed mat next to the kitchen. She saw him before he saw her. "If I remain like this, I'll fall," she told herself. "I cannot believe my eyes." She sat down on the mat. He walked towards her. There was shame in his eyes. "If the ground could swallow me now, I would not fight against it," he told himself. His legs shook as he advanced.

Finally, he sat down and lowered his head. "I'm sorry mother. I'm sorry for the pain I've caused you. I had to…"

"Thank you for coming back my son. I do not want any explanations. I am also sorry for my fear. I am sorry for wanting to keep you here. If you ever feel the need to go away, please do so. Do so, but tell me first. Tell me where you are going so that I will know where to find you if you need help. The worst thing for a mother is NOT to know where her children are."

"I am sorry mother."

"Have you heard from your brothers?

"No, I haven't."

"May the good Lord protect them wherever they are. They will be safe, I know He will take care of them. If you have faith in Him, nothing is impossible," she smiled. "I am so happy you came back. I love you my son."

"I love you too mother."

Then they drank their tea in silence.

Under
(with Prepositions)

I knew it.

I knew it as soon as I stepped onto that filthy floor that I would not stay a minute longer in that place.

If you ever go to a **double-decker hospital** and the medical personnel ask you to sleep under a bed, don't do it.

Run.

Run to wherever you came from.

Run for your precious and irreplaceable life!

Run and don't look back. Just run.

If they insist, tell them you are not a pair of old shoes. Tell them this is the most nonsensical demand you have ever received from anyone. Tell them any sane person wouldn't do such a thing, would he? Or she? Tell them you are fighting against a mighty foe and that you'd better have all the luck on your side. Tell them there is no way you will go into a boxing ring without protective gear. Tell them you will not gamble your life away under that rickety, sickly bed. Never in your lifetime! Not underneath the sun! Not underneath the moon!

If they pin you down and keep you from leaving, be bold and ask them to show you how you can sleep under the bed of a dying man. Ask them to be a good role model. We learn best through examples, don't we?

If they don't do any of this, then you are free to leave.

You are out of harm's way.

You actually have more hope of getting better going somewhere else than staying in such a shabby, dingy and dilapidated hospital.

I am glad to tell you that this is what I actually did. I, Gerald Phiri, took matters into my own hands and decided to save my life-my very own life, my precious life, my beloved life! I, Gerald Phiri, decided that my life was worthy and I would be better off outside than inside that ramshackle **double-decker hospital**.

I am actually very proud of what I did! I prized and saved my very own life! My precious life, my beloved life, my one and only life. Hey, I still have so many things to do and experience in my lifetime. Guys, I have a job that I cherish. On top of that, I have a family that I take care of, day in and day out. Who the hell will look after them if I leave this world so carelessly? So, I took the decision to leave that damn hospital. Why would I put my life into the hands of people who want to dump me under the bed of a dying man? It makes no sense!

I left that dreary hospital and I did not look back. I picked up my bags and walked out of that death trap, knowing that I would not return.

The stakes were high. My body was in a furnace- I could feel my blood boiling in every cell. My limbs felt heavy and I could barely lift my feet off the ground.

I ran across the street, even though my head was pounding and I feared I would drop onto the ground in sheer desperation. Hell no, I kept on as if some graceful force was pulling me to safety. I hung onto this lifebuoy, desperately, longingly, until I reached home.

My wife, Jennifer, was in the kitchen. She was preparing the food that she was supposed to bring me to the hospital. My son was still at school. He was in Standard Two.

" Gerald, you are out, Praise the Lord!"

"Don't take me back to that hospital," I mumbled before collapsing onto the polished floor.

There was a scream and then nothing. Darkness, oblivion, emptiness.

"How?" I asked Jennifer. " How did I end up here?"

"No fight is greater than the love that I have for you Gera. I love you Gerald Phiri and I can't imagine spending the rest of my life without you. We will get you out of here alive and kicking, no matter the cost."

Tears welled up in my eyes. It felt good to be taken care of. It felt good to be understood and recognised as a human being. It felt good to know that Jennifer loved me and that she would always stand by my side.

The pounding in my head resumed but I paid little attention to it. What was a pounding head pitted against the amazing care and love that Jennifer was providing me with?

Nothing.

A pounding head was nothing at all.
I was ready.
I was ready for the battle ahead.

Picture Perfect

(with Vocabulary
for Describing Pictures)

Anger and fear are a lovely couple, so they say. They walk hand in hand. You can easily spot them because they like to be seen and felt. She just ignores them. There are a hundred things one can do during the day and catering to the whims of this duet is something that is not on her to-do list.

Today, she is going to a place where she is most likely to meet them — the shopping mall. Such encounters are unpleasant. They take the joy out of her experience.

However, time is teaching her to tame these two savages. Their grip is loosening and she dreams of the day when she will be completely out of their grasp.

She arrives at the first shop. It does not take too long for them to show up. They are dressed in their normal gear: a stiff pair of black trousers, a stiffer shirt with a pointed collar and solemn headgear. Their dark boots are shiny. They smile as if they are about to be photographed.

A curt 'hello' follows and she feels their eyes boring into her whole being.

She is followed, as usual.

Fear settles in before it is replaced by anger. She recognises them and politely asks them to leave. They want to stay. They are here to stay, they insist. Their company is not welcome; she knows this because her body tells her so.

It is the heart that gives the first warning. It beats so wildly she thinks that she might faint. The sweat is another tell-tale sign that the two monsters have gained momentary access to her soul. A pounding headache follows and nausea threatens to turn her into a walking volcano.

Rage.

She knows she has to endure this, over and over again. But, she knows that time is her ally. It heals all wounds and repairs even the most broken of souls.

Time.

She pins her hopes on this constant law of nature.

It is what helps her to cope as anger and fear stay close to her heels, disturbing her peace, curtailing her freedom, stealing her life.

Soon, time proves to be loyal, as usual. Her ordeal is over. A breath of relief.

Sigh.

She has paid for her goods and fetched them jealously; she has thanked the personnel with a 'thank you' and a mechanical smile; she has checked that there is no stray object in her bag that will betray her when leaving the shop.

She is escorted out, half-surreptitiously, half-ostentatiously — she doesn't know if they are doing it out of goodwill or out of malice. Bad intentions. She settles for the latter. They are doing this to unsettle her, to remind her that she will always look suspicious, no matter how she looks, no matter how she talks, no matter how much money is gracing her wallet. This is borrowed land, they say. She must never feel too comfortable. She must not settle down and should be kept on her toes.

Four shops. Four escorts. Four moments when she is intensely scrutinised. Four moments when her body is subjected to unnecessary emotional pressure. Four moments when she takes the decision never to go back to that particular shop.

Courage.

It is courage that brings her back.

It is courage that tells her to take out her camera in the fifth shop.

Anger and fear are a lovely couple. They walk hand in hand. They are inseparable and most of all they like to be flattered.

As usual, they follow her as soon as she enters the shop. She smiles at them as if she is about to be photographed. They do not smile back at her. She stops and examines an object. They stop and hide behind a shelf. She walks towards them and stands next to them. They fidget with the handbags. She walks away. They stay where they are.

Her camera is still in her hand. She looks for the perfect spot to take a selfie. She makes sure that the background is pretty. Above all, she ensures that anger and fear are caught in the frame. Their faces are far, of course, because she does not want their ugliness to be etched in her mind forever.

The lighting is perfect.

Click. Click. Click. Click. Click.

Five photographs.

In the first photo, fear has a look of surprise and anger is panicking. In the second photo, fear is starting to disappear. In the third one, she is laughing and anger is long gone. In the fourth picture, fear and anger are nowhere to be seen and not even a single shadow of them remains. In the last photograph, her face is serene.

Power.

There are excellent bargains in the shop. She finds a pair of black stiletto boots. They will look lovely on her. They are picture perfect. Her sister might want some. They will come back the following week. Surely, they will.

She pays for the shoes and leaves.

It's been a good day.

Anger and fear have broken up, so they say. They walk separately, hands in their pockets. They shun the spotlight so you hardly see them nowadays. She does not miss them at all.

They are a distant memory.

Indescribable bliss.

The Handbrake

(with Punctuation Marks)

She has broken three glasses within a week; she thinks there is more to this story than meets the eye. The first time was an accident. The second time was a coincidence. The third time was neither an accident nor a coincidence. It was a premonition— a message from the universe—a warning that she had to open her eyes wide and pay attention to her surroundings.

Each incident was unique but the consequences were the same: deafening noise, shattered glass, momentary mayhem, frantic attempts to bring everything back to order, normalcy.

Lately, sleep has become elusive. She dreads the times when the bedroom is plunged in darkness and she cannot see anything. In those moments, time seems to drag by slowly. She is happy when dawn finally creeps in, softly, reminding her that the world is beautiful and that her fear is unjustified.

There is a knock at the door.

"Good morning Madam, the charcoal seller is out-side. He says that he has come for his money."

"Good morning *aMbewe*. Alright, tell him to wait a little. I will be there in a minute." As an afterthought she adds:

"Give him some of the porridge from the pot but don't put sugar in it. Things are becoming so expensive nowadays and we cannot afford to waste food in this house."

"Okay Madam," he says. "I will do that. Which plate should I use?"

"The plastic one *a*Mbewe! How many times should I remind you that the ceramic plates are only for adults and visitors?"

"Sorry Madam, I forgot. I will be in the kitchen if you need me."

AMbewe is their houseboy. He is not a 'boy' as such. He is a married man with three children. His family is in the village and this job allows him to look after them in a more dignified way. He can pay school fees, buy seeds and fertiliser and purchase a few clothes and shoes once in a while. In exchange for his salary, he cooks, washes the children's clothes, cleans their house, takes care of the garden and protects the house from thieves when the owners are not around. She does the shopping herself because it is wiser to do so. When it comes to money, you should always trust your instincts.

She takes a bath; the charcoal seller can wait. When she is ready, she goes outside to meet him. He is sitting on the veranda. It looks like he has already emptied the contents of his plate. She sighs.

"Good morning *a*Phiri," she blurts out from a distance. "*A*Mbew*e* told me that you have come for your money. Do you people think that we grow *Kwachas* on trees? Do you think that we eat mouth-watering chicken every day?"

As a response, *a*Phiri kneels and greets her: "Good morning Madam. How are you today?"

"Let's not waste time with greetings *a*Phiri! Don't pretend to be polite; I know what you want. I've already told you that the government hasn't paid my salary yet. Do you want me to steal? Have you ever seen me going to the government offices to ask for my money?"

*A*Phiri does not say anything but he has a pleading look in his eyes. He sits down defeatedly and implores her:

"Please Madam. My wife is sick and I need the money to buy her medicine. What can I do Madam? You have been promising me this money for three months, Madam. I need this money Madam, otherwise I wouldn't have waited for so long."

She has no time for this. Next time, he will say that his son has lost his leg. He always invents these stories so that people should feel sorry for him…No, she is not buying his story now…

"*A*Phiri, we all have problems and yours are not bigger than mine. Do you see that car over there? It needs to be serviced (as if he understands). You see that roof over there? It needs to be repaired. My bank account is empty and I have no money to do that. Where on earth do you expect me to find your money?"

"Madam, you promised. You have been taking charcoal from me without paying. I need the money to look after my family. I told you that my wife is very sick and I need money to buy her medicine. Madam, it's hard work selling charcoal. I am not begging; I am just asking you to pay me for my sweat."

She sighs and calls her houseboy.

"AMbewe. Prepare a bag of maize flour and give it to this man. Tell him to come back at the end of the month."

"But…," *a*Phiri tries to say something.

"AMbewe!"

The 'houseboy' rushes to the scene. He had been listening to the whole conversation. He thinks he should support the charcoal seller. He knows the wife because she comes from the same village as he does. She indeed went to the hospital to treat a powerful cough two days ago but they had nothing to give her there. She has to pay for both medical tests and medicine. He wonders what is the role of the Ministry of Health.

"Madam, it's true."

"What's true *a*Mbewe?"

"His wife is very sick and he needs money to buy her medicine."

She cannot believe it. The cheek! They are siding with each other. Do they think that she owns a silo full of Kwachas? She will tolerate this no longer.

"You know what *a*Mbewe? Don't even give him the maize flour. Tell him to leave my property right now. Enough is enough!"

There is a long silence. APhiri is still sitting on the ground. He looks as if she has beaten the life out of him. AMbewe casts comforting glances at him but does not say anything.

"Leave!"

*A*Phiri does not flinch. He remains seated. She cannot believe this! She thinks that they are taking advantage of the situation because her husband is not around. She has to put a stop to this. Period. She will teach them a lesson.

" I will call the police."

*A*Mbewe is startled and wants to say something. *A*Phiri has the lifeless look of the hopeless.

"Did you hear me? I will call the police!"

*A*Mbewe tells her it is a bad idea. She doesn't know what they might do him. Besides, look the children are awake. She wouldn't want them to witness the ugly scene to come. No, Madam should be reasonable. The best thing is to give *a*Mbewe some flour and let him leave in peace. He means no harm. He is just a poor man who wants his money back. He did not commit a crime; he did not steal from anyone.

However, Madam wants to prove a point. She is tired of these people harassing her. She wants him locked up for some time. How dare he come to her house so early in the morning to bother her about such a little amount of money! She could pay him ten thousand times!

Madam is adamant. She wants justice.

She takes out an iPhone from her skirt's right-hand pocket and dials the number of the police. The phone rings several times but no one answers.

"I will go there and fetch them myself. This man should be locked up for what he has done to me."

She goes inside the house to fetch the car keys. When she goes out, she has a couple of used shirts. She throws them at *a*Phiri.

"Here, take these. Don't bother me anymore."

*A*Phiri grabs the clothes. He is leaving.

"Where are you going?" she asks. "You are now scared, *ha*? Stay where you are. Stay right there so you can face the consequences of your actions."

"I don't want any problems Madam. Keep the money. Thank you very much for the shirts. God will take care of my family as he has always done."

"You know that you did something wrong *a*Phiri. That's why you are running away. *A*Mbewe, make sure this man does not leave this place. The police will take care of him."

*A*Mbewe does not move. She glares at him.

"Did you plan this together with him *a*Mbewe? I am starting to get suspicious…"

*A*Mbewe does not know what to do. The problem with Madam is that when she is angry, she never listens to anyone. He might lose his job if he is not too careful. He should leave *a*Phiri. He also has a family to fend for back home. One should always be prudent in such situations.

"I am sorry Madam. I will get back to work. *A*Phiri, please leave this property; don't come back please. I will lose my job if you do. Please leave."

Madam has no time to lose. She gets into her car and turns the engine on. *A*Mbewe opens the gate for her. *A*Phiri slides past the car steathily and starts running after he hits the street. Unfortunately, she spots him way too soon. Without thinking, she yells: "THIEF!!!!"

A crowd quickly gathers around the supposed culprit.

"What did he steal?" someone asks.

"Shirts," another person replies. "I think he stole some shirts from that house."

In no time at all, the mob renders its justice sense-lessly — without checking its facts, without taking a closer look at the face of the person they are judging. Is he a father? A son? A brother? Maybe a friend?

The air is filled hate and anger. Men and women cheer. Children cry. APhiri is on the ground. He can no longer talk. He can no longer breathe. He was a good man. APhiri *was* a good man.

Where is *a*Mbewe? Where is Madam?

After some time, she drives past the charred remains of the charcoal man and does not say anything. Her eyes are gleaming with contempt. Her job is not yet done. She wants full justice.

In front of her, there is a hill. The engine stops. She tries to rev it back into action but it won't flinch. What's wrong?

A few men notice that she is in trouble. They offer their help. They push the car and kick it back into life. She presses on the accelerator. She is going too fast now. The streets are crowded. She presses on the brake but they won't work. The car keeps on moving. She is now going downhill. Her heart is racing and beads of sweat gather on her forehead. She hoots frenetically to keep the children off the streets. Outside, people are shouting: "Use the handbrake woman! Use the handbrake for God's sake!"

The handbrake, of course! Why didn't she think of it???? She pulls up the lever and the car comes to a complete halt. She gets out. A crowd is gathering in protest.

"You should never leave a powerful engine in the hands of people who don't know how to drive!"

She cannot locate the exact whereabouts of the person who uttered those ominous words but he sounds very angry. She has heard this voice before. It is the voice of a desperate man who is ready to take matters into his own hands. She starts crying: "Please, forgive me Sir! You must understand Sir! The car just got out of control; I didn't do anything wrong."

The bloodthirsty crowd will hear none of it. They want to mete out their own kind of self-professed justice. When the police finally comes, there is nothing to save. Both the woman and the car have been reduced to charred dust and metal. Shards of pointed glass remain ominously on the ground. The police carefully avoid them. The soles of their shoes are full of holes and they cannot afford surgery for their feet after all…

Let Life Happen

(with Vocabulary
for Talking about Time)

He was not in a hurry to come into this world.

Weighing exactly 2.5 Kgs, he wailed into our lives one week later than his due date. The clock read 11:55 p.m. when the midwife handed me my wrinkled bundle of joy.

"Finally, he is here. You took your time, didn't you? Feed him please, he must be hungry after all these hours making his way out of your womb."

I cried with relief and general contentment as the nurse helped him nestle in my arms and take his first meal. It was difficult to feed him because he would not open his mouth and it took us a while to show him that it was all right to be there. Gradually his whimpering and fidgetting subsided and he fell into a deep sleep, curled up on my chest.

As he slept, I recalled the arduous journey that had led us here. We had been trying to have this child for years and when nature let us down, we turned our eyes towards science. It was a long process and we had almost given up. We had been longing for this baby for ages that his arrival was nothing short of a miracle.

My husband and I called him '***Tafika***': 'We've arrived'.

The road to this child had been a winding and thorny one but we'd made it. We knew that life after Tafika would never be the same. We did not know to what extent he was going to jumble up our lives.

Tafika was a beautiful child and his beauty turned heads.

From time to time, people stopped when they saw him and voiced out their wonder.

"What a pretty baby you have! Look at his skin."

He had even features that neared perfection and we marvelled at this because neither my husband and I were what you would call 'beautiful' people.

Tafika was a fragile child and his fragility robbed my sleep and peace.

I could not stop worrying about him and more than often, I rushed to his bedside at night, soaked to the bone with sweat and I would stare at him for hours on end. Later, my husband would come and take my place because we did not want anything to happen to Tafika.

Tafika was a curious child and his curiosity made my heart leap!

It seemed as if he was trying to make up for the lost time he had wasted in the beginning of his years. We followed him everywhere because he touched everything and made no difference if the object was sharp or smooth, hot or cold, dirty or clean. He endangered his life many a time and we had to make frequent visits to the hospital to mend his self.

Tafika was a fearless child and his fearlessness threatened my sanity.

The more he explored the world around him, the more anxious I grew and I became fidgety. I could not take my eyes off him. I feared for his life.

"Do not be afraid mother. I know what I am doing."

He was a child.

"He knows what he is doing," my husband said. "Nothing will happen to him. If he falls, he will rise up and dust himself."

He needed protection.

"I don't mother. I am big now. I can go to school and fight for myself. Time is too short to worry about what will become of me. I know what I want to do with my life. Let life happen."

I lost weight. He thrived. I saw him thrive and I gained weight. He liked school and he had a bunch of friends that he met every weekend at the basketball court. Every now and then, he came with a scratched knee or elbow but it was nothing worse. He grew in stature and mind. I was proud of my son.

Tafika was an intelligent child and his intelligence BLEW my mind.

It was not school intelligence. It was the type of intelligence that helped him to understand the world around him. He understood people and situations and knew when a risk was worth taking or not. He knew the value of experience and banned fear from his life.

Tafika is now a man. He has a wife and we welcomed his daughter a few months ago. My granddaughter reminds me of her father. Her beauty drops jaws and she is a bit of a restless child. From time to time, my anxiety crawls its way up from the recesses of my heart. I fear for her life because she is full of life.

Then, I catch myself fretting and sweating. I watch her take her first steps in life. I hold out my hand so she doesn't fall. I see the cold fury in her eyes. My hands drop to my side and I smile as she stumbles across the room to the safety of a chair.

"Let life happen." I whisper to myself as her mother rushes from the kitchen to comfort her.

Welcome to Migodi,
the City of Hope

(with Vocabulary for Talking about the Past and the Present)

Twenty years ago, Migodi City was a sorry sight. It wasn't even called Migodi, because Migodi means 'mines' and therefore 'wealth', doesn't it?

Twenty years ago, I'd have called this city 'Misozi'—'tears'. It would have been such a befitting name for a city that bred fear among its inhabitants and took away their joy.

It was a city where despair reigned and people lived hand to mouth, not giving a single care about the future because it had no meaning for them.

It was a city where teary children roamed the streets in quest of food which they rarely found, leaving their weary mothers worried sick at home because they didn't know the whereabouts of their children.

It was a city where very few people had access to jobs, whether they had the right qualifications or not. In fact, getting employed in the field where you trained was like winning the jackpot. It wasn't a rare sight to see frustrated unemployed University graduates sitting on the roadside and eating bananas because they had nothing better to do than complain about their misfortune. They really believed that they couldn't change their circumstances.

For women, living in Migodi was an uphill and daily struggle as you can imagine. They were homemakers, child-bearers, burden-carriers, quite the quiet sufferers and so on and so forth —life goes on. Nevertheless, they carried out their wifely and motherly duties with abnegation. They remained silent and resilient and courageous in the face of hardship. They tried their best to prepare their children for the future, especially their daughters who had to learn the hard art of appeasement. The same daughters also had to perfect the art of burying their heads in the sand because, oftentimes, it is life-saving to turn your eyes away from the thing that's constantly hurting you.

Migodi was also a city where powerful people preyed on the weak and easily got away with it because they simply could. It was a cut-throat world defined by persecutors and victims who didn't want to switch roles. It was a tough environment in which only the canniest, the fittest, and the most ruthless survived. The filthiest carried the day and the prizes of course!

To cut a long story short, no one in their right mind would have freely chosen to live in Migodi twenty years ago. It was a death trap. Curable diseases could cut your life short and you would be just another statistic to be quickly replaced by another.

Frankly speaking, who would have chosen to live in a city where food was scarce and healthcare was a luxury? Who would have packed their bags to go to a place where good education was in the realm of unattainable dreams? Who would have settled in a city where finding proper housing was a miracle? No one, I bet!

Today, Migodi is much, much different from what it used to be. Migodi has become a city of hope and a beacon of peace thanks to its inhabitants.

Things started to change when the people realised that it was only, and only up to them to transform their fate and rewrite their histories.

Migodians (as I like to call them now) have become aware that collective efforts are key to development and that there is no gain in blaming politicians for a problem that they can easily solve themselves.

Migodians have also realised that love (and not hate, let alone anger) is a powerful transformational force that can move mountains.

Migodians love their children with all their hearts and they simply cannot stand seeing them suffering. They make sure to feed their children well with nourishing and balanced food. The parents also ensure that their offspring go to good and well-equipped schools where they can learn in a nurturing environment that fosters creativity.

Migodians love their neighbours as much as they love themselves so they have stopped harassing each other for no reason at all. They now have more time to spend on developmental projects or programmes that work for the common good.

Most of all, Migodians love their loved ones and do not want to see them six-feet under. Hence, they fight tooth and nail to build state-of-the-art hospitals with modern equipment that can treat formidable diseases.

Therefore, I welcome you to Migodi, the city that I have fiercely grown to love over the years. The city of hope.

Migodi is a city that encourages personal initiative and personal responsibility.

It is a city with tarmac roads, free of potholes and avoidable accidents.

It is also a clean city with clean water and a constant supply of electricity.

To cut a long story short, Migodi is a city of abundance and filthy wealth—filthy in a good way of course.

Migodi lacks nothing thanks to the hard work of its inhabitants. Hospitals have a large supply of medicine and schools are real schools where children can really learn.

Migodi is an inspirational place with inspirational leaders. No wonder a lot of cities around the world are emulating us!

As you might have guessed, Migodi is an imaginary place of course yet its pulse beats louder in my heart by the minute. Its foundations are rooted in the very depths of my soul and I cannot turn my eyes away from this awe-inspiring place. I see Migodi when I wake up and I go to bed with its sparkling visions. Migodians have also taken real shape. Each day that passes, I marvel at their transformation. I see them grow and turn into beautiful and loving people who walk on this earth with full purpose. I want to be one of them. They inspire me.

That is the nature of hope.

THE END